Dear Pastor: A Word To The Wise

Dr. Kephyan Sheppard

TABLE OF CONTENTS

ACKNOWLEDGMENTS

This book is a labor of love and somewhat of a journal of my experiences. When our ministry launched, wisdom was rare. While there were plenty of congratulations to go around, not many were willing or available to share their experiences. This book was written to reverse that trend and to give both new and experienced pastors some tools to help them as they navigate through complicated waters.

I am grateful to the Holy Spirit for guidance in this endeavor. I honor my wife Tricina who has stood by my side each step of the way over the last nine years, and our daughter MyKayla who has sacrificed so much at a young age. Shout out to our sons, Juston and Caleb, for being awesome! I salute my comrades and colleagues in the Gospel; be encouraged and keep standing.

In memory of our loved ones who have passed on, this is for you, Fermer Lee Sheppard, Dorothy Mae Brooks, Elaina Lee, Karoline Jean Sheppard, and Raymond Wright... see you all in the morning.

FOREWORD

Dr. Kephyan Sheppard is one of the most balanced Bible teachers and pastors I know. He is a community influencer and creative thinking problem-solver. In his new breakthrough book, "Dear Pastor: A Word to the Wise," he offers practical, powerful, and fruitful solutions to a variety of challenges that pastors face on a daily basis. I highly recommend his book to ministers who are in the fledgling stages of their calling as well as to seasoned clergy who will glean fresh ideas from this volume.

Jeff Walker DMin, PsyD

INTRODUCTION

"It's Time"

"It's time" is what the Holy Spirit whispered in my ear. After three weeks of home Bible studies, it was time to launch the ministry. Being stubborn, I procrastinated and hesitated. "How?" "Are we ready?" Those were my questions. My wife and I were in a newly restored marriage, raising a two-year-old daughter, and living in a city not known to appreciate ministry. In fact, in our first year of ministry six churches closed their doors, so I was reluctant.

There we were, having completed three weeks of in-home Bible studies on the book of Acts. Our focus revolved around the church and its beginning stages from the Day of Pentecost, to the daily exchange between in-home meetings and temple worship. Our objective was to build a ministry after the heart of God, one that would show the world what the Biblical blueprint for ministry should look like.

That was our plan. God had assembled six adults and a few children to launch a small group. We were small, but we were happy, content with meeting weekly in our home to break bread and share the Word. Then the sudden, "It's Time", shook me to my core. Knowing full well the ramifications of ignoring the call of God, we began looking for a place to worship. I did my best to avoid the city that God had called me to, even attempted to find buildings in surrounding cities. All of this proved to be a waste of time and resources as eventually, God's plan prevailed.

Desert Hot Springs it is. We eventually signed a lease to move into the community senior center where we began to have worship services, and immediately served our homeless community. If you know anything about the Coachella Valley, Desert Hot Springs by many accounts has had a stigma of being a lower and upper valley. But I found solace in John 1:46. When told of the coming of Jesus, and how He would come from a lowly place like Nazareth, the question was, "Nazareth! Can anything good come from there?" I immediately substituted Desert Hot Springs for Nazareth, knowing many would ask that very question! But it was the reply in John 1:46 that stirred my spirit. A simple, "Come and see."

This book is my "Come and See". From a ministry launch to ministry growth, to pitfalls and beyond, this labor from my heart is something that I pray blesses you, the young pastor. Unfortunately for young pastors, there is not a manual or a handbook on how to effectively lead a ministry. My prayer is that this book can be one of your many resources as you forge ahead. Maybe you are here, knowing that "it's time". Take the next few moments and learn from my experiences.

CHAPTER 1

HOW DO I BUILD?

"*B*e strong and courageous, for you are the one who will lead these people..." *Joshua 1:6* Ministry launch can be scary. You begin to question things concerning sustainability. Wondering if you would be able to fill the pews or chairs and fill them with people that would give to support the ministry financially. You begin to question your worth and even your call. You start to experience feelings of inadequacy, wondering if you are truly prepared for the work. Then watch, you will experience euphoria from preaching your first Sunday as a pastor. My experience was unique because we were sharing a facility. After preaching I had the task of going to restack chairs and break down sound equipment. Set up and breakdown, which was part of my job description for possibly five to six months. What many may not know is that unless you inherit a ministry, chances are when you launch you will not only serve as the pastor, but you also become the de facto deacon, custodian, and even administrator. Because we did not have a musician, I was also the person who compiled accompaniment tracks for praise and worship. While I thank God for gracing us to function while he sent workers from the harvest, I can be honest and tell you that those days were not easy at all.

My concern was truly where would we find people to join our ministry. One thing I want to establish is that it is out of order and unethical to fish church members from other ministries. A wise man (that I met in a barbershop) once said that we pass the church on the way to church every Sunday. Meaning there are hundreds of thousands of people on the street that need to hear the Good News and be in fellowship with the saints, but we overlook them. We overlook them because those that have been conditioned to church and church service seem to be more attractive. Because of this, so many make the mistake of trying to attract people from other churches to their ministry. I do not believe that this is the will of God.

In Luke 12:43 Jesus said, "Go out into the country lanes and behind the hedges and urge anyone you find to come, so that the house will be full." This was a command to get out of our comfort zones and search for and multiply disciples. Every day in our communities, right in our own backyards, there are thousands of people who have never heard the Gospel of Jesus Christ. Let's assume some have heard the Gospel, but have yet to be invited to a church where they can be nurtured and discipled. Even beyond that, we may have hundreds that have had bad church experiences and are in desperate need of a church body. I believe that we do a great disservice to the body of Christ and our ministries by overlooking and refusing to search for these people. Often when a new ministry plants, the leaders are seen in the streets recruiting members from other churches to be a part of what God is doing there. However, that is out of order. Psalm 127:1 says, "Unless the LORD builds a house, the work of the builders is wasted. Word to the wise: a house built on dysfunction will stand in dysfunction.

The question remains, "How do I build?" Well first, pray! Any move made without prayer is a bad move. Proverbs 3:6 says, "In all your ways acknowledge Him and He shall direct your path". Prayer will calm your anxieties, provide strategy, and equip you with boldness. After prayer, the next step is to engage the community. Every city has a city council. As a new pastor, your job is to get familiar with what ails the city. You have a responsibility to position yourself to wash the feet of the city that you have been called to serve. What better way to find out how to do that than at a city council meeting? One of the first things we did was to make it a point to introduce ourselves to the city council during a meeting. During the public comments section, I approached the podium, and after introducing myself and our ministry, I offered 40 hours of community service to the city. The goal? The goal was to let the city know that we were here to serve in any and all reasonable capacities. That meeting alone caused a little bit of a stir in our city. People begin to seek us out. The thing to understand, however, is that everyone who will seek you out from that particular encounter may not join your ministry, and that's perfectly fine. Because you are building and aiming to build in a way that impacts the community long-term, you must recognize that you need members in-house and partners outside of the house as well.

The building does not stop there. Small businesses are the lifeblood of every city. Although we love to find great deals, I believe that if the church is going to serve the community, the church needs to consider the needs of the small businesses. For example, we needed flyers made. How else were we going to get the word out that we were there to serve? It would have been easier to go across the freeway and use the bigger chains, but we have two local printers here in the city. I believe that goodwill in the community goes a long way for the ministry. The seeds that we planted by patronizing small businesses allowed us to reap a harvest of favor. Acts chapter 2:47 says that "they gained favor with God and man", and I believe that man in this sense is the community itself. From our local eateries to our local print shops, to other local businesses, we sowed in business transactions to let them know that we were standing with them.

Civic engagement is another area that many churches miss out on. This is a great opportunity to allow the spiritual presence that mercy brings to be seen as well as relied on within the community. By civic engagement, I mean getting involved in the civic matters of the city. I am not one that condones or even desires to place politics in the pulpit. However, the church does have a civic responsibility to the community. There are several ways that we were able to get involved without being directly involved in politics. One of the first things we did was to meet with our local police chief and strategize. We were coming off of a period of civil unrest that our nation had not seen in a while. There was distrust between the black and brown communities and the police. There was racial tension on our high school campus and beyond. We sat down with our local police chief and we discussed the police community forum. A forum where the police chief would be able to introduce some officers, go over protocols, and discuss the things that the community needed from his perspective. However, this was not a one-sided conversation. We also made sure that the residents were able to discuss what was going on and the issues that they saw with our police department. These forums went a long way in improving the relationship between our local police and the residents within our community. Additionally, we hosted several debates for those that were running for local offices, we had open forms with our mayor and even held forums with our school district personnel. These events were meant to establish the ministry as a presence in the community.

Now that we have planted seeds with city staff and leadership, let's take it to the streets! Now, I need you to transition your mind frame from the traditional thought that says that a church is effective based on the number of people sitting in the pews. Success for ministry cannot be gauged by numbers on Sunday, but by the numbers of lives that are impacted for the rest of the week. Taking words directly from Jesus himself in Matthew 25, we are to care for "the least of them". Now mind you, I have not even gotten into worship service yet. Why? Because attempting to reach those that are lost, especially those in the streets is a priority for me in this season. The numbers of those that are homeless are beginning to increase at a substantial rate. We ought not to forget to care and serve even those who many look down upon. When we launched, the very first thing that we did immediately following our first Sunday service was drive around the city looking for people to feed. That became a staple of our ministry, to the point where now we are known as the ministry in our region who will do all that we can to care for our homeless population. There is a major blessing in giving, especially when giving to those who have nothing to give back (Luke 14:14).

Finally, you have a golden opportunity to build from within. Here is the revelation: people WILL join your ministry. Go ahead and get excited. Know that when you cast your net, fish will gather. Now, the key is understanding how to tap into the potential of those that are coming. You will have uniquely gifted people walking through the doors and become a part of your ministry and an immediate assignment to create pathways for them to serve.

Upon uniting them with your ministry, there should be some type of ministry form that not only details their contact information, but an area for them to explain their gifts and talents. From that point, it is up to you and your leadership team to create an atmosphere conducive for them to serve.

At this point, you should begin to identify who your leaders will be. Remember, the goal is to make disciples, or as one wise man once told me, "give the ministry away". This process is key because you cannot carry the ministry burden alone, you are not strong enough nor were you called to do so. You have to remember that from day one, Jesus had a vision to make the disciples "fishers of men" (Matthew 4:19), and with that in mind, your charge will be to equip and empower leaders. Building now shifts to an inside job as you begin to spend time with and pour directly into this leadership group. As we know, Jesus touched many, walked with twelve, and had an inner circle of three. This leadership team may not be large in number, but they benefit greatly from your pour. Establish regular leadership meetings, engage them and allow them to challenge you, and most importantly keep the vision in front of them.

From civic engagement to community outreach, to weekly in-reach (searching for those in the ministry to disciple), building is a multi-faceted process. It is your job to cast vision and set the tone and culture of the ministry you were called to lead. A word to the wise:

Leave people alone! This is a season where we will see the unchurched run to the church. We must understand that we cannot clean fish before they are caught. In other words, build the church with the Word, being led by His Spirit, while operating in love, and God will do the rest.

CHAPTER 2

WHAT IS THE VISION?

Then the LORD answered me and said: "Write the vision and make it plain on tablets, That he may run who reads it. *Habakkuk 2:2*

I love Webster's definition of the word vision. According to Webster, vision is "the ability to think about or plan the future with imagination or wisdom." Vision serves as a guide, a motivator, and even inspiration. Vision remains alive even when it seems everything around you shows signs of death. Vision will keep you returning to the pulpit and in the community week after week. I believe David would testify that there is a life-sustaining power in vision. In Psalm 27:13 he said, "I would have lost heart, unless I had believed that I would see the goodness of the Lord in the land of the living." Amid frustration, his vision was that he would see the goodness of the Lord while he was alive, and that vision kept him from fainting and throwing in the towel. Trust me when I tell you, there have been some seasons where all I had to hold on to was the vision that God promised me... and that was more than enough.

But the question must be asked, who are you as a church? What is your purpose? Why do you exist? Maybe you know the answers to these questions. Maybe those closest to you know the answers to these questions, but what about the person looking for a church home? What about the non-believing philanthropist looking for a charitable organization to give to? Trust me, it happens. Will they be able to easily identify your purpose and vision? If your answer is no, chances are you have yet to formulate and present mission and vision statements. A mission statement explains why you exist. Not to be confused with a vision statement, which explains your purpose and what you aim to achieve. Now obviously winning souls to the Kingdom is the end game, but how will you accomplish such a feat? Sunday morning services? Outreach endeavors?

Pastor, everyone you encounter that asks about your ministry should be able to easily determine your why (mission statement) and your how (vision statement). Due to the tragic circumstances surrounding the COVID-19 pandemic, it has been reported by Google that online searches for salvation and things concerning Jesus have skyrocketed (Shellnutt, 2020). This is a good sign because people who have never been a part of the church are seeking something. Many need what you have to offer, but in many cases, you won't have all day to explain to them why it is that they need to fellowship with you. Mission and vision statements are concise descriptions of your ministry, its purpose, and its vision.

Now for those within the ministry, the vision needs to be cast and kept before them for some of the same reasons listed above.

Everyone wants to be a part of something, and most of us want to be a part of something bigger than ourselves. What is even more exciting is to be a part of something bigger than ourselves and to realize that we can play a large role in it. Because ministry involves different types of personalities, backgrounds, and even perceptions, sometimes the road may be a little rocky. But having a vision statement before the people will prove to serve as a rallying cry to get everyone back on track. A consistently presented vision statement will serve as a reminder, something to keep everyone focused.

You as the leader have to be the number one spokesperson/cheerleader for the vision. That vision needs to follow you everywhere you go; it needs to proceed from your mouth in nearly every conversation; and needs to work its way into nearly every sermon. When people in the church see you, they need to see the vision. When people in the community see you, they need to see the vision. When colleagues see you, they need to see the vision. This is when you become creative. Your social media posts need to point people back to the vision. Get some t-shirts made. Record some videos. People are more likely to get involved in your ministry and organization when they have a clear and concise vision placed in front of them. Even a non-believer will see that your vision has the potential to impact the community at a greater level and will get involved.

A couple of years ago we had the opportunity to purchase our sanctuary. We were so excited because when we began our ministry sharing the senior center in our city, this was a major blessing in seven short years. From the senior center, we were able to acquire a small office space. The space was so small that we could only fit 56 chairs inside of it comfortably, and we quickly grew beyond those 56 chairs. After a couple of run-ins with potential code enforcement violations, we were able to acquire an old warehouse to hold our worship services in. The warehouse was a blessing to us because it was more room, more space, and opportunity. We were even able to convert parts of it to create children's rooms and executive offices. After a short while there, we were presented with the opportunity to lease a traditional sanctuary. An old Lutheran temple had become available and after meeting with the board we decided to move forward. We stayed there for three years. A lot of blood, sweat, and tears were poured out revitalizing that building. It was home to us. For the first time, I was excited to call a place home. I just knew that would be the future of our ministry. But just before the three-year mark, I received a phone call letting us know that a new church building had become available. The building was only two years old and had been foreclosed. I knew the building well, as I watched while it was being built, and I took several tours of the building. Never in a million years did I imagine that we would occupy that particular building. Needless to say, we jumped at the opportunity, and that opportunity came with quite a price.

Now here we are at the beginning of a fundraising campaign. We had a substantial amount to raise to enter escrow. Now most people that know me know that I am a man of great faith, but even those of us with the gift of faith have some limitations and doubts at times. We had seen God perform miracle after miracle in our ministry from financial, to health, and even seeing the hand of God add time to a particular individual's life. But we had never believed God for anything this big before. Before I tell you the rest of the story, I want you to remember chapter one. From day one we made sure that we served our community, and we kept the vision in front, not just in front of our church family, but in front of our community as well. Our assignment has always been to serve the homeless population, from meals to even temporary shelter plans. Over the years we have worked with our county officials to designate a portion of our church grounds to house the homeless during the inclement weather seasons and have been known for the duration of our ministry to be one to consistently look to serve the "least of them". Now, I tell you this because I want you to keep it in the back of your mind as you read what happens next.

Our escrow schedule was split into two payments, the first due in December and the second in April. The Lord simply told me to cast the vision to the people and let them know what His plans were for the property. Let me add that this property was tailor-made for our mission as it came with over three acres of land attached to it! So, there I stood on a Sunday morning just before I delivered the sermon. The day before, several of us had gone to the church property to "scout the land" and unlike those in Numbers 14, all of us had the same good report. I began to explain to the church where the Lord said we were headed, and praise erupted in our sanctuary. We immediately began packing and preparing, and by the grace of God, we were able to submit our first part of the escrow payment on time!

Our celebration was short and sweet because we knew mountain number two (the second and final escrow payment) was upon us and that date was approaching fast. We resumed our in- house fund-raising efforts, and I kept the vision in front of us. Each meeting, small group, worship service, casual conversation, the vision of the new church building, and the adjacent land was at the forefront of every conversation. We sold BBQ dinners, held fish fries, and yard sales. I mean we did it all! At the end of our rope, with three days left, we found ourselves $20,000 short. Faced with the prospect of losing everything, my faith never wavered, but I did begin to ask God, "Ok, what now?!?!?" As a leader, you set the tone. If those you lead see you rattled, chances are they too will become rattled. I prayed. I needed guidance and strength, I needed the Holy Spirit to give me the courage to stand before them and let them know that we fell short. God did just that, and believe it or not, praise erupted around the Sanctuary with many proclaiming that nothing was too hard for our God!

Forty-eight hours before I had to make the call to the escrow agent, my phone was ringing off the hook from people who were not a part of the ministry but valued the work of the ministry. They had watched from afar as we fed and clothed the homeless, worked with our police and city officials, and impacted our community for the better. Each of them asked, "How much do you need?", and each made significant contributions. By the end of that day, we were over the amount that we needed to close escrow!!!

You may get tired of speaking it but trust me people are listening. They may not share your Facebook posts or show up to your outreaches but trust me they are watching. Plant the seeds of the vision everywhere you go. The harvest will spring forth at the most opportune time. The miracle that God performed for us happened only because the community knew the vision!

CHAPTER 3

DON'T BURN OUT

"**T**hen Jesus said, "Let's go off by ourselves to a quiet place and rest awhile." He said this because there were so many people coming and going that Jesus and his apostles didn't even have time to eat. *Mark 6:31*

Dear Pastor, you cannot do it all. No matter how anointed you believe you are, no matter how charismatic you are, and regardless of your level of intelligence, you are a human being. Four years ago, I wrote my doctoral dissertation on pastoral suicides. If you recall, between the years 2013-2015, there seemed to be a wave of pastoral suicides. Pastors preaching their first service and choosing to end their lives before the second service begin. As heartbreaking as that was for me, I begin to look for patterns and similarities in each case. Almost 70% of those cases are appointed to the pastors suffering from depression (Gaultiere, 2021). Now, we could be naïve and act as if depression does not affect the body of Christ, but most of us know that depression is in the pews as well. The shocker however was the source of the depression. Nearly every one of the pastors who committed suicide not only shared depression in common, but they also shared burnout. Burnout is an emotional, physical, and mental condition characterized by exhaustion. This exhaustion is usually caused by elevated and prolonged stress. The symptoms are noticeable, and they revolve around feelings of being overwhelmed, emotionally drained, and frustrated concerning time-constraints.

Trust me, I know what it's like. It's like I can almost see the look in your eyes, you are ready to go out and change the world starting with your community one block at a time. But allow me to caution you to slow down. Allow me to take you on a journey, my five-year whirlwind. It was 2014, just two years after we had planted. I had attended a growth seminar that changed my life. The seminar challenged me in unimaginable ways. I was convicted for what I perceived to be underachieving (hadn't finished my college degree). I was charged to go deeper in the Word and to consider the strategic side of ministry. Immediately after the seminar, I enrolled in a Bible college. Keep in mind, this is the year 2014, the ministry was growing and I had just committed to spreading myself extremely thin because "I can do all things through Christ that strengthens me" (Phil. 4:13). Every other Saturday I would wake up at 6 a.m. and embark on a 90-minute commute to campus, where I would be in class for seven hours.

After earning my bachelor's degree, I began to have a few health issues. It was the end of 2014 when I developed a sinus/respiratory illness that not only limited my breathing but would have me on large doses of prednisone steroids. The migraines, the weight gain, the consistent mood swings, and yet I pressed. I went into the master's program, albeit handicapped respiratory wise. In the middle of the program, I was told that I would need an emergency sinus surgery. This surgery would become number one of five! Surgery after surgery, injection after injection, I continued to act as if I was superman. I believed that a sign of weakness or vulnerability would hurt or hinder the church and those that were a part of it. I became my own source of strength because I refused to "sit down". It's amazing how we can trust God for everything and everyone else but refuse to do so as it pertains to rest for ourselves. For whatever reason, my lack of discipline to rest was fueled by ego, innocent ego. I say innocent ego because I actually believed that if I rested, the church would fail. Dear Pastor, I don't mean any harm, but allow me to share with you what the Holy Spirit shared with me, "YOU ARE NOT THAT IMPORTANT!" Pride will prevent you from resting when necessary, creating an over-exaggerated self-importance. Ministry was not designed to be done alone. Word to the wise from Proverbs 16:18, "Pride goes before destruction."

The disciples had just seen the hand of God as they fed 5,000. They had become so consumed with ministry that they failed to care for themselves. Ministry can draw you in just like that. Almost like a high, you become obsessed with serving and working in the vineyard to a point where your overall health can become the least priority. There I was dealing with a debilitating respiratory issue, preaching 52 Sundays a year and teaching over half of our weekly Bible studies. The next few years would be a whirlwind of achievement as I would go on to earn my master's and doctorate's degrees, record and release two albums, plant a second ministry, and on top of all that, I was designated to the office of Bishop in the summer of 2018.

The year 2019 opened and despite all the wonderful things the Lord had allowed me to accomplish over the previous few years, I had a day of reckoning health-wise that January. The sinus and respiratory issues had become so severe, to the point where the headaches required that I have major surgery. The surgery was scheduled for July, and coincidentally my consecration for the elevation of Bishop was scheduled to happen in a month. Now, as I fast forward to the end, the surgery was a success although extremely dangerous. According to the doctor, I lost large amounts of blood while on the operating table. Needless to say, nearly three weeks later I stood in and was consecrated as a Bishop of the Lord's Church. There is a picture that encapsulates the entire moment. The picture is so powerful because it is the moment before my episcopal garments were placed on me and my face is full of tears. There is a moment where I just apparently exhaled and whenever I think of that moment, I recall what the exhale meant. That strong exhale was a moment of worship. In that moment I thanked God for preserving me in my rebellion. I knew that I should have rested and taken care of myself, but I rebelled because I made ministry all about me. That exhale was a moment of praise, thanking God for keeping His hand on me through a difficult surgery and a declaration that by faith, I would be healthy and whole moving forward.

Dear Pastor, a word to the wise, it is a marathon and not a sprint. You cannot pour from an empty cup! Listen to the Holy Spirit and REST! You will have to develop a discipline to honor your time, carve out time every week to tend to yourself. One of the things that give me an escape is working out six days a week. I am in the gym taking care of my body physically and relaxing in my mind psychologically. Doing all that you can to take care of your health is so important. Understand that a majority of the congregation will not be conditioned to think of your needs. For many of our congregations, most will see us as a problem-solver without taking into consideration that we have problems of our own.

I know the feeling. I know the passion for the call. Because of your love for Jesus, your heart is huge, and your desire to serve and help is unmatched. But understand that sometimes the enemy can use the thought of ministry work as a subtle way to distract us from the main thing. One man once told me that we can get so busy doing the work of the Lord that we forget all about the Lord of the work. There is an abundance of statistical data to support what I am about to say, so walk with me here. The under-shepherd needs time with the shepherd. The shepherd feeds the under-shepherd what He desires for the sheep to be fed. If you the pastor don't have time with God, you will end up leading from a place of "you" as opposed to being led by "Him". This principle is reinforced throughout the scriptures. Jesus Himself had to get away to pray. Moses had to leave the people behind and climb up the mountain to speak with God. As a leader, you will have to separate yourself to hear from God. Additionally, statistics show that those that are overwhelmed in ministry lack in their prayer and devotion time (Gaultiere, 2021). Leader, Pastor, how can you lead if you are not able to hear from God?

CHAPTER 4

BUILD, PREPARE, EMPOWER, AND TRUST THE STAFF

"**B**ut as the believers rapidly multiplied, there were rumblings of discontent. The Greek-speaking believers complained about the Hebrew-speaking believers, saying that their widows were being discriminated against in the daily distribution of food. So, the Twelve called a meeting of all the believers. They said, "We apostles should spend our time teaching the word of God, not running a food program. And so, brothers, select seven men who are well respected and are full of the Spirit and wisdom. We will give them this responsibility. Then we apostles can spend our time in prayer and teaching the word." Acts 6:1-4

Growth will happen. The question is, how will you handle the growth? Will you assume all the responsibilities, stretching yourself while neglecting yourself and your family? Or will you seek God for a harvest of qualified leaders, build them, prepare them, empower them, and trust them with the vision? These questions are so incredibly important to the new pastor. The tendency is to assume that if you don't do it, either it won't be done or it won't be done correctly. Living in Southern California I have seen my fair share of traffic accidents. Our freeway is cluttered daily with people who seem to just have no regard for other drivers. One of the common denominators of many traffic accidents and collisions that I have witnessed is that usually, someone would cause the collision by drifting out of their lane. Well just when you thought I was talking about traffic; I'm talking about ministry as well. Imagine how many accidents and collisions we could avoid in the church if everyone just learned to stay in their respective lanes. Well, pastor, it is your responsibility to appoint these leaders, and designate these lanes.

Building involves constructing something by placing parts in order. There will be members of your ministry that have leadership qualities. They exhibit them from week to week, and they are unaware of the leadership potential that they have inside of them. The potential is something God placed inside of them, and you are the leader that God placed for them. Being the leader, you have a responsibility to not only help them identify the gift(s) but to expose them to opportunities to build them as well. Remember, building involves putting together multiple parts. The first part that you need to add to the building recipe is your spirit. The worst thing you can do is appoint a leader over an auxiliary or over a part of the staff and that leader does not have your spirit. It creates almost a two-headed monster, a form of division. How will you know if they have your spirit? Time and observation. I believe this is one of the reasons the Apostle Paul said, "Lay hands suddenly on no man, neither be partaker of other men's sins: keep thyself pure" (1 Tim. 5:22).

In the Pentecostal church, it appears that leadership development is something that is always desired but never delivered. I have seen it time and time again. The senior pastor preaches every Sunday, teaches all the Bible studies, and completes all the leadership legwork. Meanwhile, the ministers, elders, and associate pastors are just charged to sit in the pulpit and be prepared for opening and closing prayers, if even that. There is something incredibly wrong with this picture. The template that Jesus established was one that showed that we need to give the ministry away. Meaning that we are to identify those that God has called us to lead, and then pour into them.

Remember the ultimate goal is to send them out so that they can make disciples themselves (Matt. 28:16-20). However, they are unable to do that if they have not been properly trained or equipped. Create the culture now that establishes regularly scheduled ministerial staff meetings. During these meetings challenge them to grow, get deeper into Scripture, go lower into service, and develop a stronger prayer life. Prepare them for the event that if something catastrophic happens and you are not available. Your ministers should be able and well-equipped to carry on the work of the ministry should you become unavailable. Teach them the duties that come along with the office to avoid a situation where they grow into a person with a title but no function. We all need to understand that the ministry should be built on the Word, but not a particular voice.

Prepare! By prepare, I mean to get them ready to be used. I remember watching a football game years ago. The team's quarterback went out with an injury, and the little-known backup had to come in and finish the game. The backup had not had any practice reps with the starters, had never seen real game action. However, to his credit, he had a cerebral approach to the game. He knew the ins and outs of the playbook. He knew where everyone was supposed to be on the field, and he was great with reading the defense before the ball was snapped. However, he had no actual experience. So, although the coach was confident, the team had quite a few concerns, and rightfully so. The backup goes into the game and on his first snap, he throws an interception. Obviously, the backup returns to the sideline and the coach gives him some encouraging words and slaps him on the helmet, and sends him right back out there. He immediately throws another interception, and by this time the crowd had lost its patience. At the end of the day, the box score revealed that this was one of the worst quarterback performances of recent history. You see, the issue was not that he wasn't intelligent enough. Nor did it have anything to do with his ability to grasp the offensive playbook, or even understand the complexities of a defense. The issue was that he had no real experience, and since he had no real experience, he never should have been expected to perform in the first place. Now let us transition from football and get into the actual ministry. You want to trust your leadership staff. You want to trust those that you have developed and poured into. You want to believe that they would be able to stand in your stead should anything happen to you. Therefore, they need real-life opportunities.

So, what do you do? Let's first establish the fact that Sunday mornings the pastor should be preaching. Unless you are on vacation, or sabbatical, you should be preaching on Sunday mornings. Reference back to the last chapter, there will come seasons where you need to rest. During those seasons, your staff needs to get those opportunities. Now being the leader, you realize that not everyone has a Sunday morning gift. Some are simply gifted for the mid-week Bible study. But some will have a gift for Sunday morning, an ability to stand flat-footed and preach the gospel. On your rest times, they need to have opportunities. One of the most demoralizing things that you can do to your staff is to bring in an outside voice every time you are not available to preach. But here is the truth, if the staff is not properly prepared then it may possible that you have not effectively poured. Word to the wise: ask God to help you identify the deficiencies each member has, then seek Him for strategy concerning each individual.

Empower your staff. Give them the authority or power to do their jobs. The empowering process begins in public view. The people need to witness you empowering those that will lead with you. If you notice, I did not say they will lead FOR you, rather WITH you. We have a twisted view of the relationship between those that are leading, and those being led. I will admit that most of this twisted view has come from poor theology. Without sparking a potentially much- needed debate, I want us to remember that in John 15, Jesus calls us friends. Being that those that you lead will serve as your associates in ministry, it will be important for you to validate them openly. When a leader who has not been validated openly attempts to lead, there is a potential for distrust among the membership. Like the Apostles in Acts 6, you need the ability to focus on the Word and the vision. Constantly putting out small fires will diminish your ability to effectively lead.

David Huntoon put it this way, "Empowering builds confidence in their capacity to execute your collective mission and goals, establishes essential trust in an organization, and creates the secondary level of leadership necessary when you are not present for key decisions so that the organization continues" (Huntoon, 2021). You empower your leaders for their confidence. There is nothing like knowing that your leader believes in you. Additionally, you empower to build that next level of leadership. This is necessary because certain things should never have to reach your desk. Empowered leaders are confident leaders, and confident leaders are powerful leaders! Jesus told the disciples that they would do greater works than He did in His earthly ministry (John 14:12). The key however was in His address to them known as the Great Commission, "Then the eleven disciples went to Galilee, to the mountain where Jesus had told them to go. When they saw him, they worshiped him; but some doubted. Then Jesus came to them and said, "All authority in heaven and on earth has been given to me. Therefore, go and make disciples of all nations, baptizing them in the name of the Father and of the Son and of the Holy Spirit, and teaching them to obey everything I have commanded you. And surely, I am with you always, to the very end of the age" (Matt. 28:16-20). Empowerment involves acknowledgment (of their charge), assignment, and delegated authority. I believe in your leadership staff, and so should you.

Finally, there is trust. Micromanaging is a form of leadership that has to have its hand in everything. Micromanaging sets up a culture of distrust, insecurity, as well as a feeling of inadequacy among those that are being led. Put yourself in the position of one of the members of your leadership staff. Imagine how difficult it would be to make decisions knowing that this may be diminished because you were consistently hovering over their shoulder. Trust says that there is a firm belief in their reliability and ability. Trust speaks to their character when people know that they have earned the trust of the leader. It builds confidence and crushes all doubt. Trust says, "I am appointing you to do this. I know that you are well able, and I cannot wait to see the growth."

But I will caution you. Trust me when I say this, it is not easy to trust. The ministry in itself is almost like your baby, and I can recall many sleepless nights where I delegated something, and I was worried about its success. I will never forget the first time that we went away, and ministry had to go forth. I had become so accustomed to being at everything for the duration of whatever event, that the first time I was away I was nervous and ashamedly afraid. I need you to understand that while you may be trusting your staff, you are putting the ultimate trust in the Lord. Trusting Him to know that His vision will not suffer and that your leaders will effectively carry on in your absence. This takes spiritual discipline. I was given this analogy a while back, and I feel it applies to this topic. My grandmother once told me that if you go to a family cookout and everything tastes the same, it is likely that one person cooked all the food. Your ministry should reflect the diversity of the people in the room. Your ministry should reflect the special gifts and talents that everyone possesses. If your hand has to be involved in everything, everything will sound like you, and depend on you. And we have already talked about the danger of everything revolving around you.

Catch this…for the shepherd, the staff was an instrumental tool to help deal with the sheepfold. With the staff, the shepherd had the ability to reach and touch sheep beyond his arm's length. This is key when you place it within the confines of your ministry. Your staff will be an extension of you one way or the other, why not do all you can to make sure they represent God and their leader well?

CHAPTER 5

BALANCE

"For everything there is a season…" Ecclesiastes 3:1

There is a word that needs to be taught in ministry circles over and over. That word is balance. Balance has two definitions according to Webster's. The first says, "an even distribution of weight enabling someone or something to remain upright and steady." And the second reads, "a condition in which different elements are equal or in the correct proportions." Pastor, it is imperative that you find a way to have an even distribution of the weight of ministry, family, health, and even leisure. These elements should be approached with a focus on equality.

Sometimes I sit back and wonder how my marriage survived. I short-changed my wife because I was so focused on the church. I have heard it said that many preachers have an adulterous affair on their wives with the church. As funny as it sounds, that is true as it was in my case as well. My life was consumed with the church and I justified it by stating that I was simply doing the will of God. Pastor, it is not the will of God for you to forsake your wife for the church. My good friend Demont Jefferson laid something out for me so profoundly nearly a decade ago. He said, "Kephyan… That church is God's bride, Tricina is your bride." That was a revolutionary moment for me and life in general. Because for the first time I saw that I had neglected my duties as a husband to pursue what was right for the church. Proverbs 3:5 instructs us to trust in the Lord with all of our heart, and I discovered that I had a lack of trust. I just assumed that I had to do everything for the church and trusted that my marriage would be fine. It should have been the opposite. I should have put everything into my marriage, trusting the Lord to make sure His church was fine.

So, I was that husband. That pastor who pursued selfish ambition under the guise of doing the Lord's work. Pastor, do not allow your marriage to suffer the way mine did for years. By the grace of God, we were able to recover, but it was not easy. As you read this, I want you to keep a few things in mind concerning the battles your wife will face. First, your wife has to compete with your legacy and anointing. It is assumed that because she is your wife, that ministry life should come easy. Unfortunately, for many, she is expected to preach like you preach and move the way that you move. In fact, it is also assumed by many that because she is your wife she is automatically called to preach. She is often expected to carry the oil that you carry simply because she is married to you. Your wife will have to deal with the fact that she has to share you with those that may not even value your anointing. Therefore, you will have to go the extra mile to hear her and address her concerns. Finally, your wife has to deal with the fact that while she is standing with you, she still has to find her voice. These three battles can easily be won with your compassion, patience, and support. Remember this, your marriage is your most important ministry, because your marriage reflects the beauty of the gospel. Look at the symbolism! Just as God unites us to each other, He unites us to Him with Christ. Allow her to find her voice in the Lord without pressure.

Trust me, the blend of marriage and ministry is not easy, but you can succeed. Thank God for the Holy Spirit! There will be disagreements, seasons where you won't see eye-to-eye, but your list of ministerial priorities begins with your spouse. The prophet Amos in chapter three verse three asked a rhetorical question. "How can two walk together unless they agree?" Your spouse is not only your life partner but your partner in ministry. Your spouse should be your primary support system, prayer partner, and covering. Word to the wise: allow your spouse to be what God designed them to be in ministry, not what you prefer, have seen, or perceive as being ideal. One of the struggles we had was that I thought my wife should be the first lady that I saw growing up. You know, the big hats, pretty dress suits, sitting in the corner and running the women's department. However, as we progressed in ministry, I discovered that a major source of contention between us was that I was trying to squeeze her into a role that was not her. She is uniquely gifted; unlike anything I have ever seen before.

Once I removed myself and allowed God to be God, we all noticed that she began to flourish. Why is this important? Because a struggle in the church will birth a struggle in the home. For home life and ministry life to flow, they have to be synonymous. Meaning that they both have to be balanced to a point where they prosper together. Now keep in mind, just as they can progress together, they can regress together.

Your children are another priority. Imagine lending yourself for Sister Jones' son and his behavioral issues, Brother Marshall's daughter for her lack of respect issues, and others, all while missing your own child's recitals and other activities. How do you think your child would feel? Is it possible that your child may feel that the lives and activities of other children are more meaningful to you than theirs? This is an area where I feel I have succeeded. I was adamant about making sure our daughter felt my love AND my presence wherever she was. We have three children total, and our 11-year-old is the one with us full time, and she sees everything!

The realization that your children see everything cannot be understated. Their awareness and attention to detail can prove to be both negative and/or positive. It is common knowledge that children often replicate the behaviors they witness from their parents, and when they become adults, they repeat many of them, good and bad. In ministry, that rule is also magnified. I remember years ago our daughter decided to mimic her parents. She acted out what she saw in us from her eyes. It was hilarious, but then hours later, I began to consider some of the things that she portrayed. I wasn't necessarily happy with the type of man that I was presenting to her. Nothing major to those who always look for scandal, but something as simple as when it came to portraying me, she was staring at her phone nearly the entire time. And then I begin to see that same pattern with her as she got a little bit older and she finally had her own phone. I believe that subconsciously she was showing me that it disturbed her when we were out at the movies or at dinner and I would always have my phone in my hand. However, it goes beyond that.

We want to show our children the proper way to worship and serve the Lord. We have to be careful with the amount of the ministry that we bring home. One of the worst things ever is to know that a child has lost respect for a member of the church simply because they overheard the parent negatively speaking about them. Additionally, there have been multiple accounts of children vowing to avoid the church altogether simply because of the impact that the ministry had on their childhood. So many have testified to the fact that they never had a "full time" father or mother because their father and mother chose the church over them. Now, some may say that's just perspective, but keep in mind that since your first priority is your family, their perspective matters.

I did say, however, that this is one area where I feel like I have succeeded. Our daughter is now 11 and since she began middle school, every Friday regardless of the weather, work, or anything else, I made sure that I was at her recess as a volunteer. Our father-daughter dates never really had any hiccups, and I make concerted efforts to ensure that she sees that her father is here for her. However, now that she's getting a little older, the dynamics have changed a little. (Fathers if you have a little girl you know exactly where I am right now.) But even with changing dynamics, there is nothing more important than making sure that I'm a present figure for her. Once I was able to balance the two: being a husband and being a father, ministry just seemed to get a little bit easier. For years I was an effective father, pastor, and leader, but an ineffective husband. And over those years I saw the hand of God move mightily but I would come home and feel as if the house was divided. Again, because my family is my first ministry, eventually I had to sit down and have a talk with God and figure out where I had gone wrong. His response to me was directly in the chest. I had neglected my family for his bride. Pastor, all I'm trying to tell you is to find balance. You can effectively serve the church and all your family, but it's going to take discipline. If there is anything I could tell you to take away from this is LEAVE THE CHURCH AT THE CHURCH SO HOME CAN BE HOME!

Finally, there are matters of health. The Pastor has a stressful position. The pressures sometimes go unnoticed and even unknown. You will have sleepless nights. You have seasons where you feel inadequate. You will have the pain and frustration of people that you once covered desiring to uncover you. You will struggle with holding grudges and unforgiveness. You will pour tirelessly sometimes into vessels that have holes in them. There will be seasons where you will be overwhelmed and overworked and only appreciated once a year. I will say this, your mental and physical health is a priority. Sometimes we get so involved in helping and praying for everyone else through their problems, that we forget that we have problems of our own. Those problems tend to stack and build and eventually wreak havoc on our physical and mental state. For your mental health, be sure to form an accountability circle. People who you can talk to without judgment, who can pray for you, and can be there to restore you should need to be restored. The statistics are glaring and speak loudly to the fact that most pastors lack real and meaningful friendships, primarily because they feel as if they cannot trust anyone (Grudem, 2018). I can tell you from experience, friendships and accountability circles will save your life. You cannot be vulnerable with your congregation, because for some if they see your vulnerability, they will attempt to disqualify and discount your capacity to lead. Therefore, you must have a group of people that you can just lean on in times of crisis, and when you need guidance.

Your physical health is just as important. When I was growing up, it appeared that every preacher had a weight problem. And I never understood why that was acceptable, especially when seeing them eat after church (LOL). Not to throw stones at anyone, however, I saw so many dying from hypertension, diabetes, and other ailments that I feel could have been resolved had they had a healthier lifestyle. It is far too easy to fall into a habit of maintaining a poor diet. After a long day of meetings, sermon prep, church business, etc., it just seems like the fast-food restaurants are calling your name. I can tell you that I have done it plenty of times, finish preaching a sermon, and immediately crave a cheeseburger. It wasn't until I turned 40 that I realized that I had to be careful concerning the things that I put in my body.

I recommend keeping fruit in your office at all times. Fresh fruit does wonders to replenish your body after preaching. I would advise you to be sure to stay hydrated, water is always preferred. Take care of your immune system! Vitamin C, vitamin B12, vitamin D, elderberry and zinc, and more. Your immune system will fight for you in the cold and flu seasons. Lastly, work out. I don't expect everyone to be me. I have been known to be somewhat of the "Incredible Hulk" when it comes to the gym. Not because I'm super strong, just because I'm dedicated to being physically active at least six days a week. I still have body goals, but my workouts are no longer about my body goals, rather my health goals. Pastor as I said earlier, this is a marathon, not a sprint. You have to treat your body like the fighting machine that it is. Let's get healthy together!

CHAPTER 6

CHURCH HURT: WHEN THE PASTOR HURTS

"If an enemy were insulting me, I could endure it; if a foe were rising against me, I could hide. But it is you, a man like myself, my companion, my close friend, with whom I once enjoyed sweet fellowship at the house of God, as we walked about among the worshipers. *Psalm 55:12-14*

By now you should understand that pastoring is not for the faint of heart. I remember when I went to my bishop at the time and told him that I was called to pastor. The Honorable Bishop C.E. Simmons looked me in the eyes and his words were, "Son, either you are called…or you're crazy!" He said it with a chuckle, and then that chuckle turned into a serious frown. He shared some things with me concerning his nearly five decades in ministry, but it wasn't the highs that stood out to me. When he began to share some of the lows, those were the things that stuck with me on my drive home. I wondered how a beautiful assignment can bring so much pain and frustration. I was perplexed for a while but then I recalled the apostle Paul's writings in Philippians 3:10-11, "I want to know Christ and experience the mighty power that raised him from the dead. I want to suffer with him, sharing in his death, so that one way or another I will experience the resurrection from the dead!" That day in January 2012 revolutionized the way that I approached the pastoral ministry. That was the day that I realized that this was truly a dirty job. For years we glorified the pastorate and made it attractive. We made it so attractive that frauds and hirelings went out and planted churches because the position seemed glamorous. They went after a title without knowing the function. They ran after the prestige but had no purpose. Pastoring is not about the once-a-year appreciation, or the name recognition, and the privileges that may be associated with it. Pastoring is about leading the sheep, nurturing the sheep, and protecting the sheep. I always tell people to read the fine print, because in the fine print you will find the details that many overlook. As Paul said in Philippians 3, there is suffering attached to this work.

Church hurt has become a hot topic of late. There have been various conferences, podcasts, and more all geared toward exposing the way the church has hurt countless numbers of people. And usually, in these conferences, there is a one-sided approach to address the heart. The heart is always portrayed as if it comes from the leadership to the people. Now, I am not one to diminish anyone's experiences, perceptions, and hurts. I have been on the opposite end of that spectrum as well. I have not always been in leadership and I have been hurt by leadership, so much so that I vowed never to be that leader. But there is another side to church hurt. There is a church hurt from the congregation to the leader. Yes, even the leaders are hurt in ministry.

I remember the first time that I lost a member. I learned a lesson in this whole ordeal revolving around the fact that they are not "my" members to begin with. It was our second year in ministry, things are going well, and we were growing. We had an individual that was on fire for the Lord and the ministry. Wherever that individual had to serve, they did so with diligence and excellence. We were in normal communication with the individual, weekly check-in's and discussions to encourage and build. The individual's family was growing in the ministry and all was truly well. Then suddenly one Sunday after a special presentation the individual just stopped coming to church. We called and our number was blocked. We emailed and there was no response. So, we just prayed. It was almost as if this individual just dropped off the face of the earth. Months went by and I was watching a Facebook live broadcast and I saw the individual serving as an usher at another church. I had several emotions, and I will admit some of them were not Godly. Initially, I was angry, and that anger then turned into sadness and confusion. The individual that we poured into greatly just up and vanished. I held a grudge for a month or so, and I was reminded of the scripture in 1 Corinthians 3:7, "It's not important who does the planting, or who does the watering. What's important is that God makes the seed grow", and that's where I received my deliverance. From that point on I was able to see that I was emotionally involved to the point where I made it about me instead of it being about the will of God. It was our job to plant, and it was someone else's job to water. And it was up to God to add the increase. Needless to say, that was the first hurtful situation I experienced as a pastor. But I grew, and instead of being bitter, I became better. There is nothing you can do to avoid a situation like this, but in teaching the people you have to stress that there is a proper way to leave. One thing I stress is we are to arrive with celebration and leave with grace.

There was another time in ministry where I as a leader expected someone to serve in a leadership role within the ministry. This individual hit the ground running hard, but something wasn't quite right. I was so excited to have helped, but I did not listen to the Holy Spirit's voice. The Lord kept urging me to be careful, cautious, and to take my time with this individual. But again, I was just excited to have help. As time went on, the individual became rebellious concerning my leadership. I begin to notice open disrespect at staff meetings and private conversations where my character was assassinated. This began to be exposed to me. Dear Pastor this will happen, I urge you to nip it all in the bud.

I am not an oncologist, but from what I know about cancer I understand that the best method of attack is a direct aggressive one. There is always a fear that if cancer isn't treated early and aggressively, that it could spread. Cancer happens in the church as well. And in this particular case, I didn't listen to the Holy Spirit's voice as it pertained to slowing this down. And I did not listen to the Holy Spirit as it pertained to dealing with the issue. For whatever reason, I attempted to sweep it all under the rug. Living in Southern California I have to see the news every year about wildfires breaking out along the coast. With every fire, there is an announcement to show how much of the fire is contained. A fire that has a high percentage of containment is one that isn't a threat to spread anymore. However, a fire that has a low amount of containment is a threat to spread everywhere. Pastor, when you have these types of situations in your ministry, allow me to speak a bit of wisdom into your life: "What's not confronted will not be contained." By the time I got around to addressing the disrespect from the individual that I had placed in leadership, much damage had already been done.

The individual that I trusted with the ministry that God had given me to lead, had attempted to form a coup. It was obvious that the individual was planning to try and steal the ministry right from under my feet. Second Samuel tells a great story of how David had to deal with his son Absalom attempting to steal the kingdom. The story that I'm sharing with you and the story concerning Absalom have quite a few parallels. The individual's tactics evolved from private criticism to open disrespect. I had a chance to deal with it then, but I sided with remaining peaceful. But because that situation was not dealt with properly, the open disrespect turned into an all-out rebellion. That all-out rebellion quickly evolved into an attempt to split the church. This is where the church heart comes into the situation. Those who I led faithfully and consistently sided with an individual who they barely knew as my character was being assassinated. Even after the individual was exposed for who they were, I found that the damage was irreparable. Ministerial friendships were broken and destroyed, at no fault of my own. That hurt was from the fact that the benefit of the doubt was never extended to me. As I mentioned earlier, there is a certain level of pain from watching those who you have loved and covered attempt to expose you.

Your family will be a target for some. Your lifestyle will be an attack for others. But remember the apostle Paul tells us in Ephesians chapter six that we are not wrestling against flesh and blood. You have to understand that the enemy is looking to discourage you. He is looking to convince you to throw in the towel. He will use anyone and anything to convince you to walk away. One of the most hurtful experiences is to know that you will likely have to lead while you bleed. But this isn't news, Jesus Himself has given us the example. The writer of Hebrews 12 spoke on this by saying, "Therefore, since we are surrounded by such a huge crowd of witnesses to the life of faith, let us strip off every weight that slows us down, especially the sin that so easily trips us up. And let us run with endurance the race God has set before us. We do this by keeping our eyes on Jesus, the champion who initiates and perfects our faith. Because of the joy awaiting Him, He endured the cross, disregarding its shame. Now He is seated in the place of honor beside God's throne. Think of all the hostility He endured from sinful people; then you won't become weary and give up." This is a passage of scripture that you will need to either commit to memory or place somewhere on a wall in your office. I promise there will be times where you will want to throw in the towel. I cannot tell you how many times I have thought that it would be easier to just go and serve in a ministry as opposed to leading one. But thank God for His strength.

Matthew 26, Jesus spoke these words, "My soul is crushed with grief to the point of death…" The gut punches from the ministry will knock the wind out of you. There will be Sundays where you just will not want to get out of bed and face the congregation because of the hurt. You will have moments where people ask you to pray for them, but in reality, you really would like for them to pray for you. You wonder how people can be so selfish to take advantage of your time. You will become exhausted because you will feel as if you have wasted oil. Your friends won't understand you, and your family may forsake you. But despite the church hurt, you cannot quit! Jesus spoke from His agony in Luke 22:42,

"...yet not my will, but yours be done". And that must be your continued prayer.

A final note. Ask Him to show you early on the difference between a lost sheep and a rebellious one. You have an obligation to leave the 99 and chase after the one sheep that may be lost. The lost sheep is in a world of trouble and likely won't realize it. What does the sheep look like? Well, that situation is one where you won't have peace in your spirit until you know that the sheep is secure, even if it happens to be in another ministry. A true Pastor hurts when any sheep has gone astray. Now the rebellious sheep? That one you pray for. You pray the same prayer that was prayed for the prodigal son. This prayer is that they just come to their senses and return to the Father. There is an extreme danger for you going to rescue one that has rebelled. The time that I almost ruined my life, my ministry, and my family chasing after a rebellious sheep is a Lifetime movie all in itself. One that I never want to relive.

Jesus said, "Father forgive them, for they know not what they do". These are truly words to live by. The life of the under-shepherd is a life of forgiveness. You will not be able to effectively lead sheep with bitterness in your heart. I will leave you with this if the source is bitter, then all that the source provides is contaminated.

CHAPTER 7

REMEMBER TO FORGET

"And no one puts new wine into old wineskins…" *Mark 2:22*

Dear Pastor, remember the traditions. Respect the traditions. But do not be locked into the traditions. I believe that we are in a season where major adjustments need to be made, and COVID-19 helped reinforce that belief. This is truly a season of innovation. Innovation means to make changes and introduce fresh ideas. This season, the innovative mind will be the mind that is at the forefront in terms of gathering souls into the kingdom. I am third generation Church of God in Christ; I grew up as the bridge between the old church and the new church. Early on in the ministry, I realized that a lot of the methods that I tried to operate within my ministry were merely a duplicate of what I saw in the church growing up. What I also noticed was that many of those methods were not conducive to growth, nor were they effective. You have to decide based on the evidence of fruit not on tradition or preference. You will need to learn to evaluate yourself and your leadership style. Whatever has been implemented that is not fruitful will need to be cut away. This process will be painful and uncomfortable. It will require you to unlearn some of the things that you want to hold onto, but it will prove to be beneficial. Let's remember, as with any other organism, whatever does not adapt eventually dies.

Speaking of Mark 20:22, I'd like to apply that scripture to methods in the current church. Methods that include virtual small groups, one on one discipleship, and beyond. Keep in mind, that the message will never change, but methods will. Just as the landscape of business has changed, the landscape of the church is changing. For those that enjoy cinematic entertainment, we have witnessed a consistent approach to elevation over the last 15 years. What began as a Friday night perusing the aisles of a Blockbuster location evolved into a home delivery DVD selection from Netflix. That Netflix innovation evolved into a drive-up DVD selection at Redbox. Seeing the trend and gazing into the future, Netflix then backed away from the home delivery of physical DVDs and created an in-home streaming service that has been duplicated by a new wave of service providers. I circle back to Netflix because I want us to look at Netflix as a visionary. Nearly a decade ago the executive staff of Netflix saw that the world was changing. They decided to position themselves as an agent of change and remain a leader in the home entertainment industry. Because of their innovation, the market opened up to other subscription services such as Hulu, YouTube TV, Disney+, and more. And now due to the unintended consequences of COVID-19, movie theaters have closed, and Hollywood executives have begun to offer blockbusters screenings via in-home streaming, a service that Netflix pioneered. Why is this relevant to a book concerning pastoring? Because to be effective, YOU will have to embrace a pioneer's mentality and thought process.

The model of discipleship and evangelism have shifted, and you must shift with them. The days of "packing the church" for any and all programs may be behind us, and in recognizing that fact, we have to embrace the newness with zeal and make the most of this new season. A few statistics for you to consider:

• In 2017, more than half of Bible readers used the internet (55%) or a smartphone (53%) to access biblical texts, a significant increase from 2011 (37%, 18% respectively) – Barna Group.

• More than 70% of nonprofit communicators consider social media one of their most important communication channels – Nonprofit Marketing Guide.

• Almost 85% of churches use Facebook – Lifeway Researchers.

• The average click rate is 115% higher for church emails that include at least one social media link – Anthony Coppedge: Focused on Church Health.

• 54% of Christian millennials watch online videos about faith or spirituality – Barna Group.

Do you see the trend? Social media and online platforms have become a necessity in the body of Christ. COVID-19 has shown us plenty, and without getting off-topic, I will say that about this book, COVID-19 has shown the need to adapt, adjust, and implement social media strategies to keep in touch with our congregation and continue gathering virtually. The old-school tent revival may have evolved into the new social media meeting place. Now trust me when I say, I cannot wait until we can have an old-school tent revival again, there is something in me that still feels that they are necessary. However, with so much uncertainty sweeping the land, and the lack of security for many that are battling health issues, we ought to make a shift. We do not have the time to wait for things to return to normal. The time is now. The opportunity is here, and there is an urgent need.

A recent article from Religion and Diplomacy stated that "In March 2020, the share of Google searches for prayer surged to the highest level ever recorded, surpassing all other major events that otherwise call for prayer…" People are searching for the truth now more than ever. The pandemic globally has caused spiritual eyes to be opened, and now those that were lost, thirst for answers. But the question is how will they be reached? I believe that God is forcing us to leave the old wineskins, the old methods, and lean on His guidance to become innovative. From your local ministry, you are now able to reach across state lines and international waters. Pastor, while setting your budget for evangelism, invest in an online presence. Facebook pages, YouTube pages, Instagram accounts, websites, whatever you have to do take the limits off. This is a season of great opportunity, and great opportunity should be met with great expectation.

I don't take for granted that some who may be reading this book are not senior pastors. A large portion of this book applies to you, because even being a supporting leader, there are principles that still apply. But I want you to understand that your leader needs your support. Remember the battle at Rephidim in Exodus 17? The Israelites were able to remain victorious as long as their leader Moses was able to hold his arms up. But eventually, his arms grew weary, and they began to lose the battle. The Bible says Aaron and Hur then went and placed Moses on a rock, and each held up one of his arms for the battle to be won. Whether you are grooming to be a senior pastor yourself, or you are called to stay in with your senior pastor, I understand that your pastor's arms will get tired, they will grow weary, and you can play a huge role in preserving them and keep him from throwing in the towel. Stand with your leader and be in position to hold up his/her arms.

Dear Pastor, trust God. Step out and launch. Advance the Kingdom. As I close, I want to remind you of the profound words of the apostle Paul from Ephesians 3:20, "Now to Him who is able to [carry out His purpose and] do superabundantly more than all that we dare ask or think [infinitely beyond our greatest prayers, hopes, or dreams], according to His power that is at work within us, to Him be the glory in the church and in Christ Jesus throughout all generations forever and ever. Amen."

These were not just my thoughts; they were actual experiences. I endeavored to offer wisdom and insight to what you are either currently dealing with, or preparing to step into. Ministry hurts. Ministry is uncomfortable. Ministry is often inconvenient, but ministry is rewarding. You are not just called to preach, you are called to nurture, guide, correct, and beyond. You will need to stay in the presence of God to continually hear His voice. I urge you not to become enamored with the praises of people because those praises can soon turn to criticisms. I tell our church often that if you live for their approval you will eventually die from their criticisms, and to focus on Paul's words in Galatians 1:10, "Obviously, I'm not trying to win the approval of people, but of God. If pleasing people were my goal, I would not be Christ's servant."

I pray for your continued strength. I pray that the Holy Spirit continues to provide you with the innovation needed to grow His church in this season, and I pray for your wholeness. Do not measure growth in terms of numbers, but in terms of reach. Finally, I encourage you to find time for yourself. Your ministry will grow at the pace of your personal devotion to God, your survival depends on you remaining in His will. Remember, you cannot pour from an empty cup.

Grace and Peace

REFERENCES

Gaultiere, B. (2021, January 20). Pastor Stress Statistics. Retrieved February 01, 2021, from https://www.soulshepherding.org/pastors-under-stress/

Grudem, E. (2018, February 01). Pastors Need Friends Too. Retrieved February 01, 2021, from https://www.desiringgod.org/articles/pastors-need-friends-too

Holy Bible, New Living Translation. (2015). New Living Translation. https://www.tyndale.com/nlt/ (Original work published 1996)

How Successful Leaders Use Empowerment to Build Trust and Excellence. (n.d.). Retrieved February 01, 2021, from http://www.davidhuntoon.com/leaders/successful-leaders-use-empowerment-build-trust-excellence/

New International Version Bible. (2011). The NIV Bible. https//www.thenivbible.com (Original work published 1978)

Shellnutt, K. (2020, December 03). 2020's Most-Read Bible Verse: 'Do Not Fear'. Retrieved February 01, 2021, from https://www.christianitytoday.com/news/2020/december/most-popular-verse-youversion-app-bible-gateway-fear-covid.html

www.ingramcontent.com/pod-product-compliance
Lightning Source LLC
Chambersburg PA
CBHW061343120726
48001CB00002B/1004